This Coloring Book Belongs To :

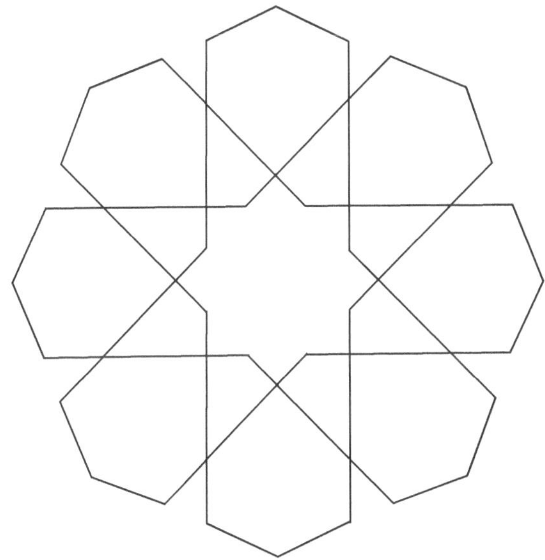

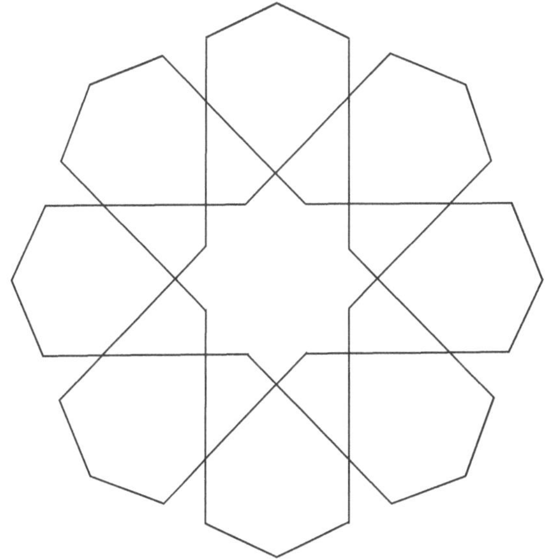

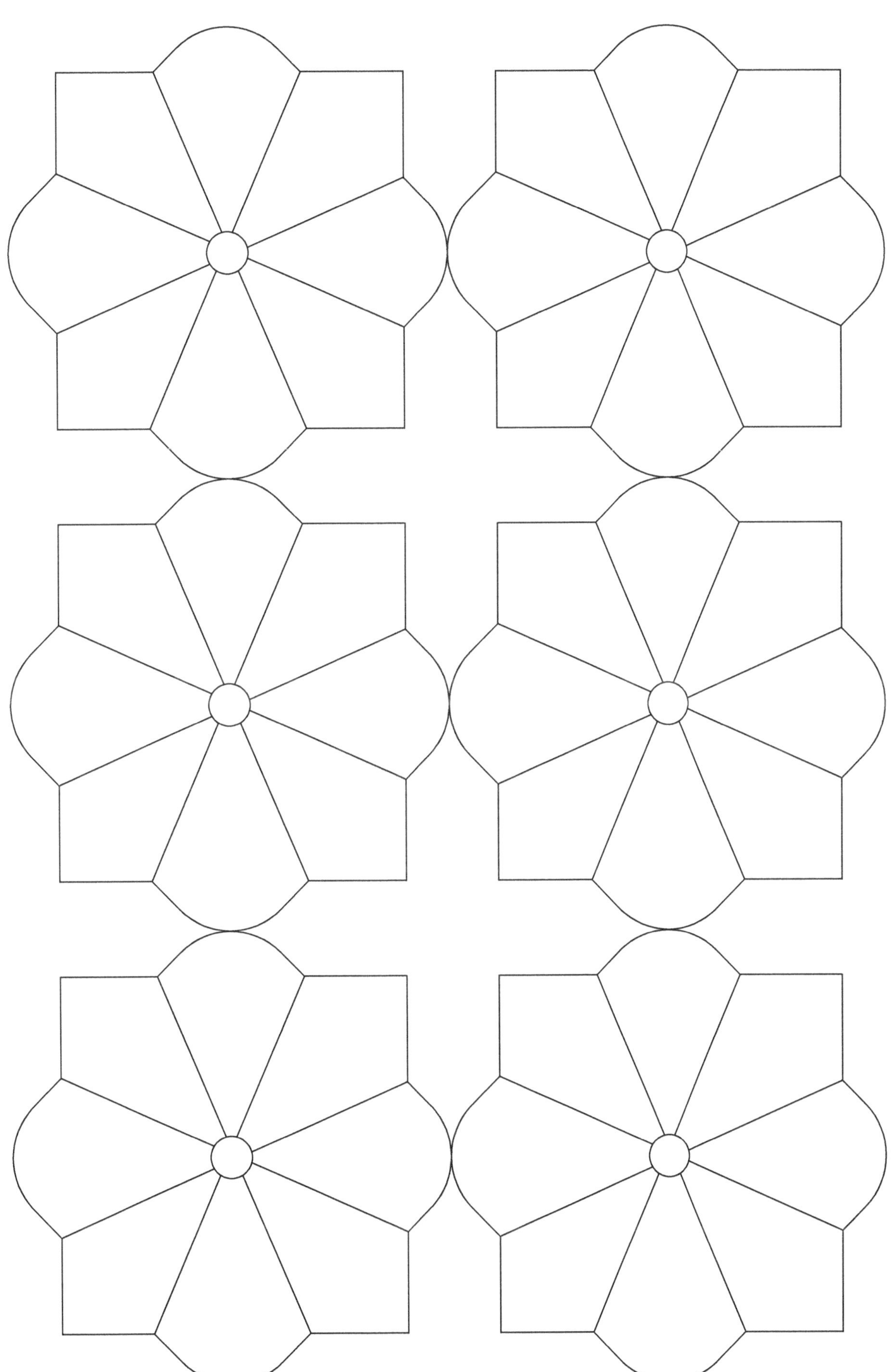

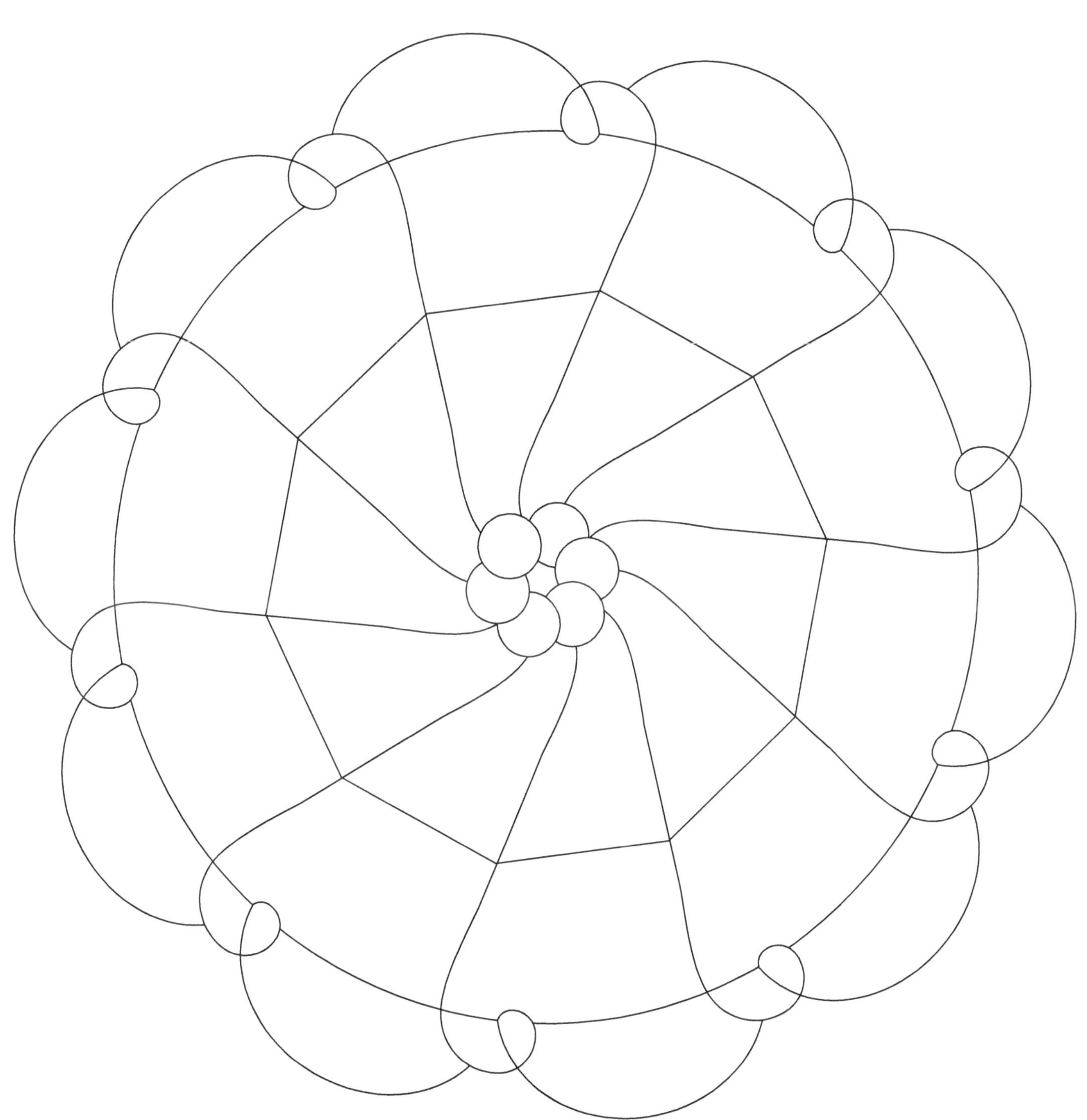

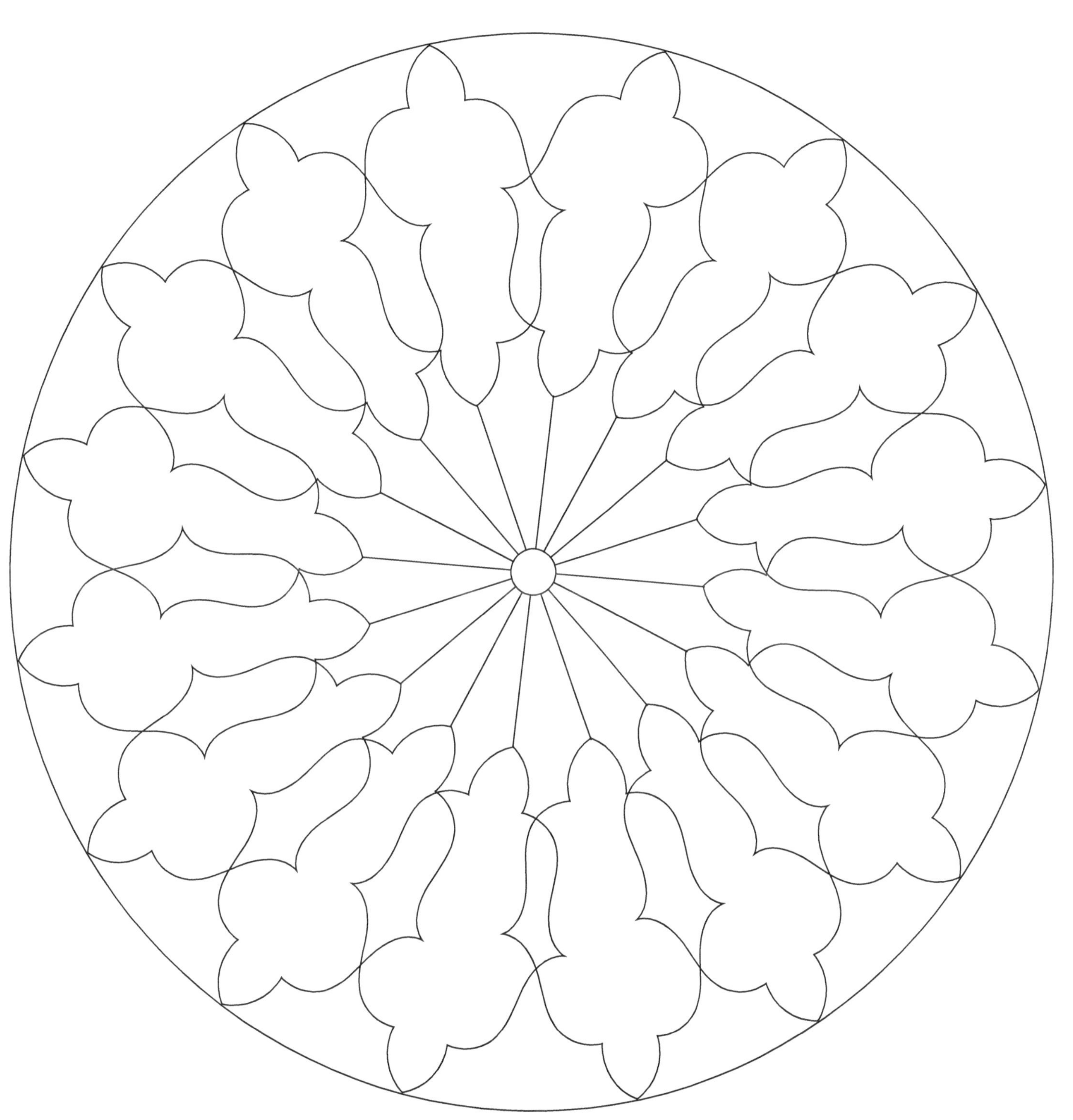

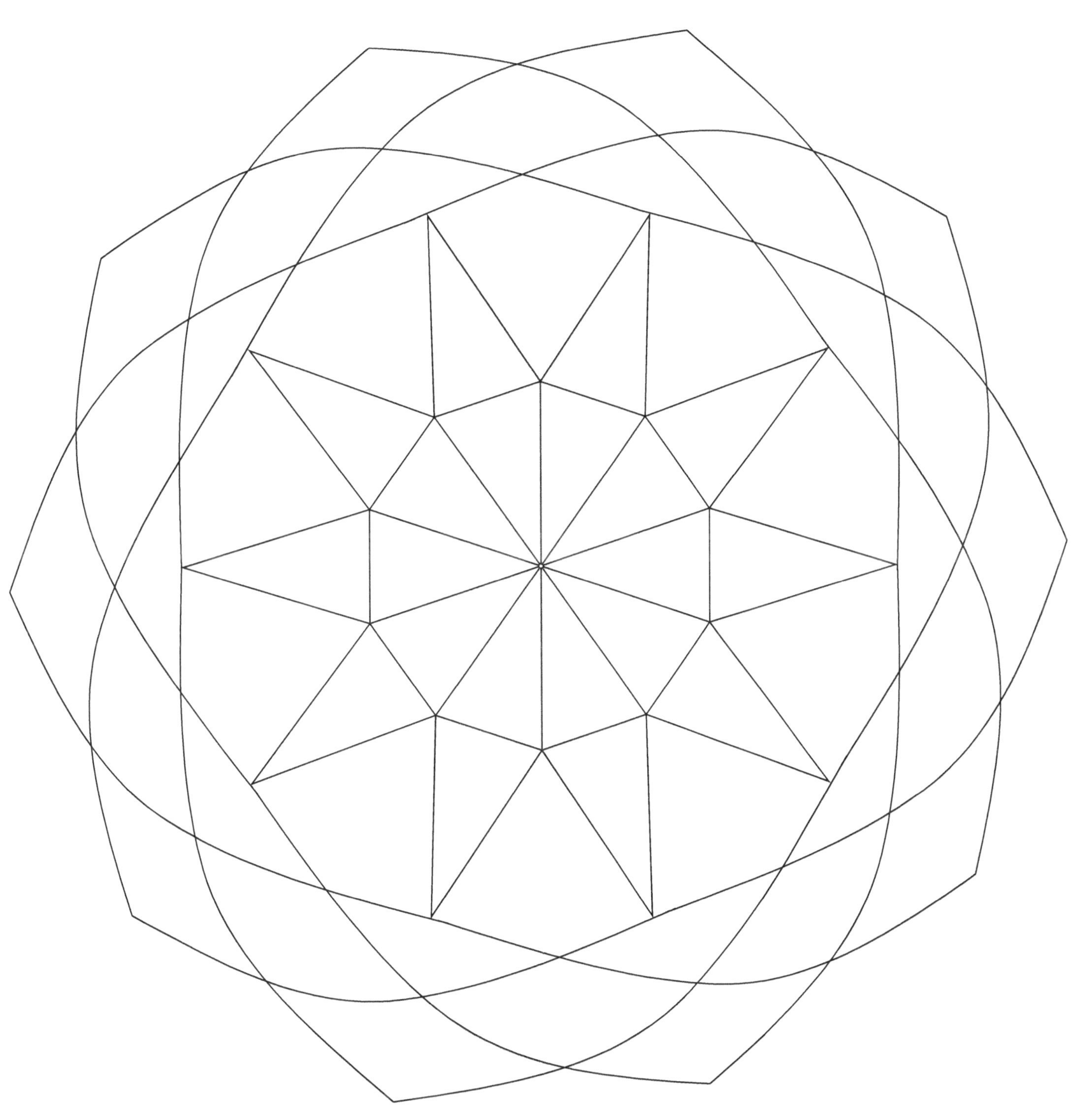

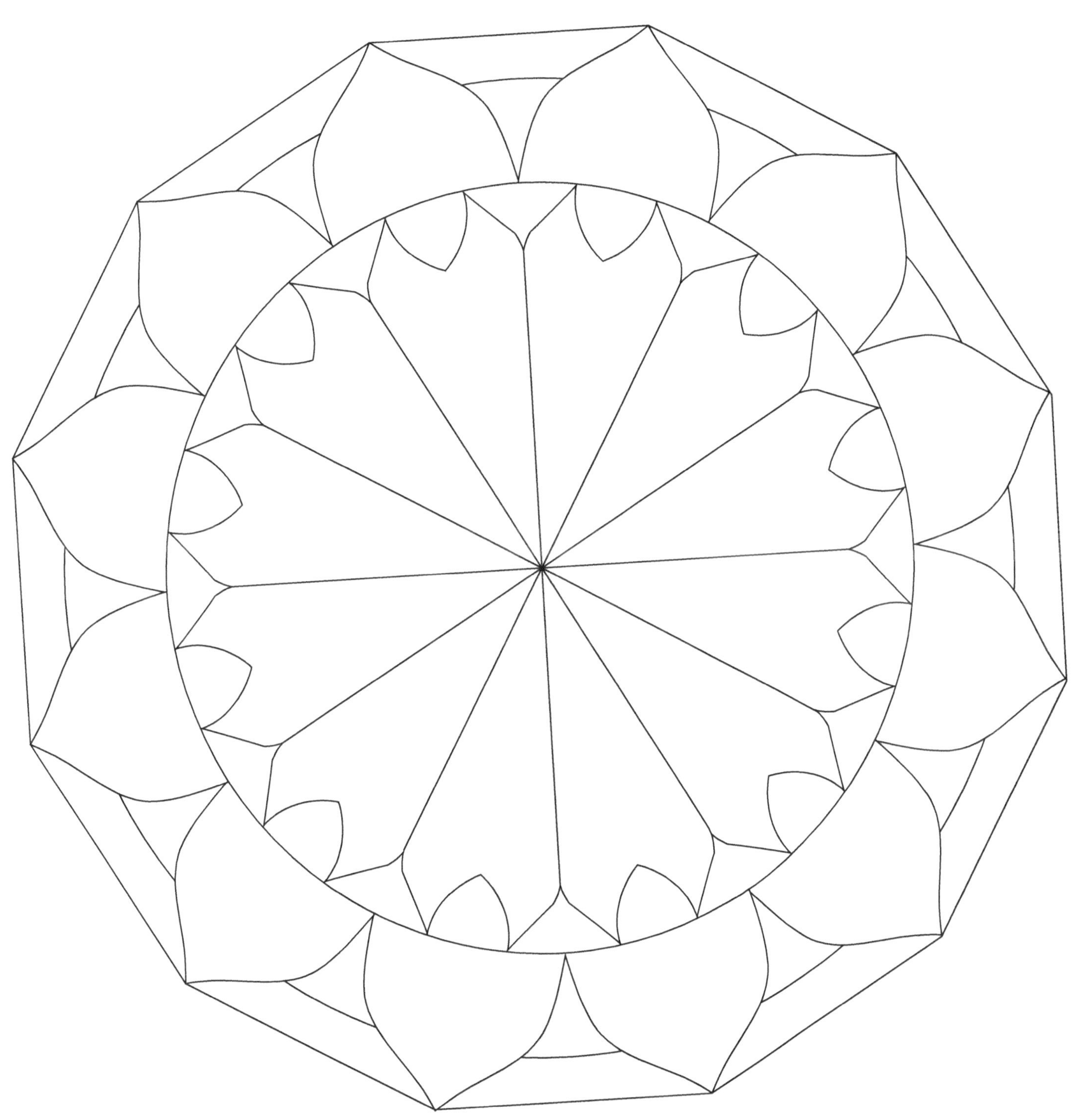

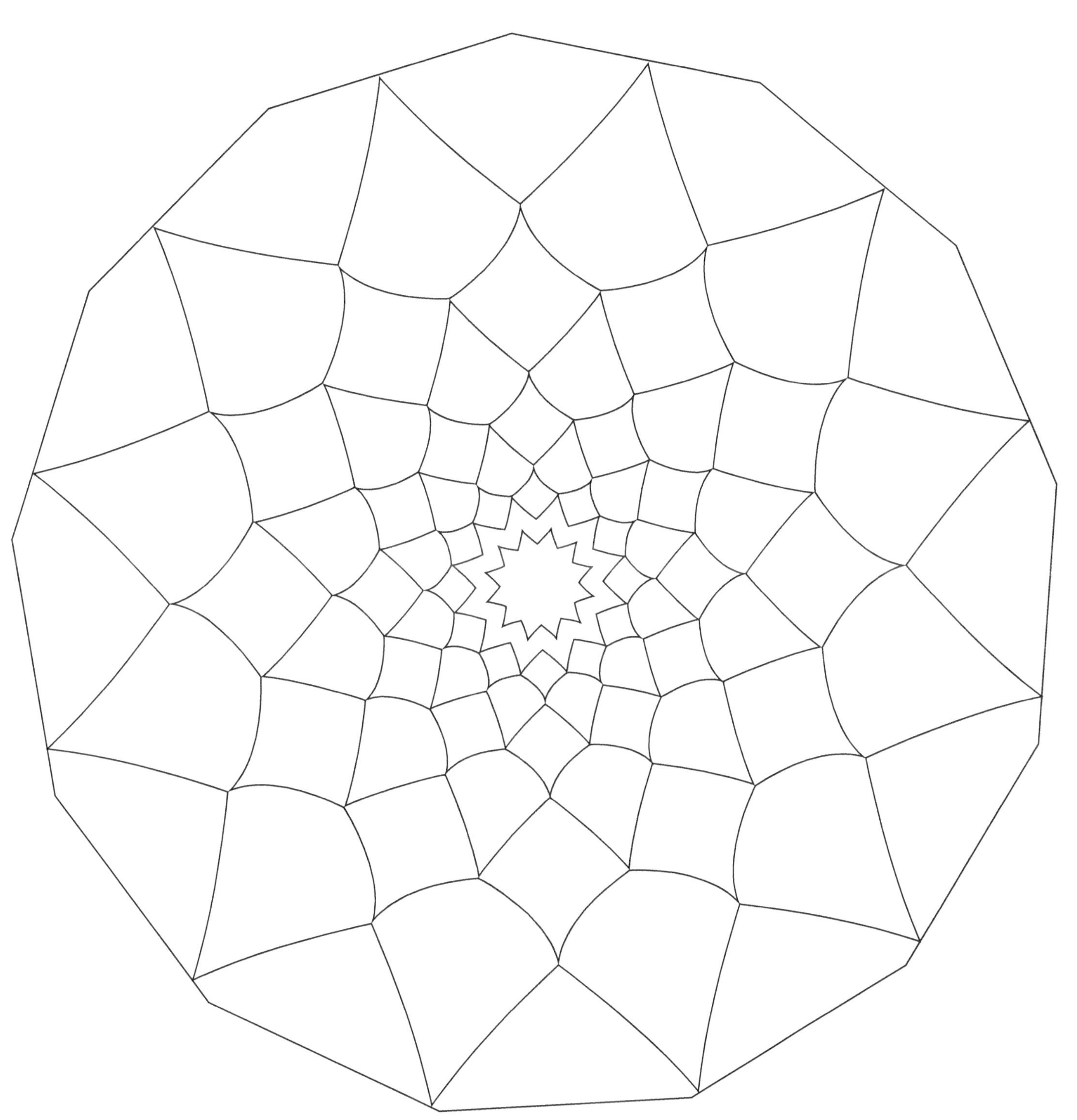

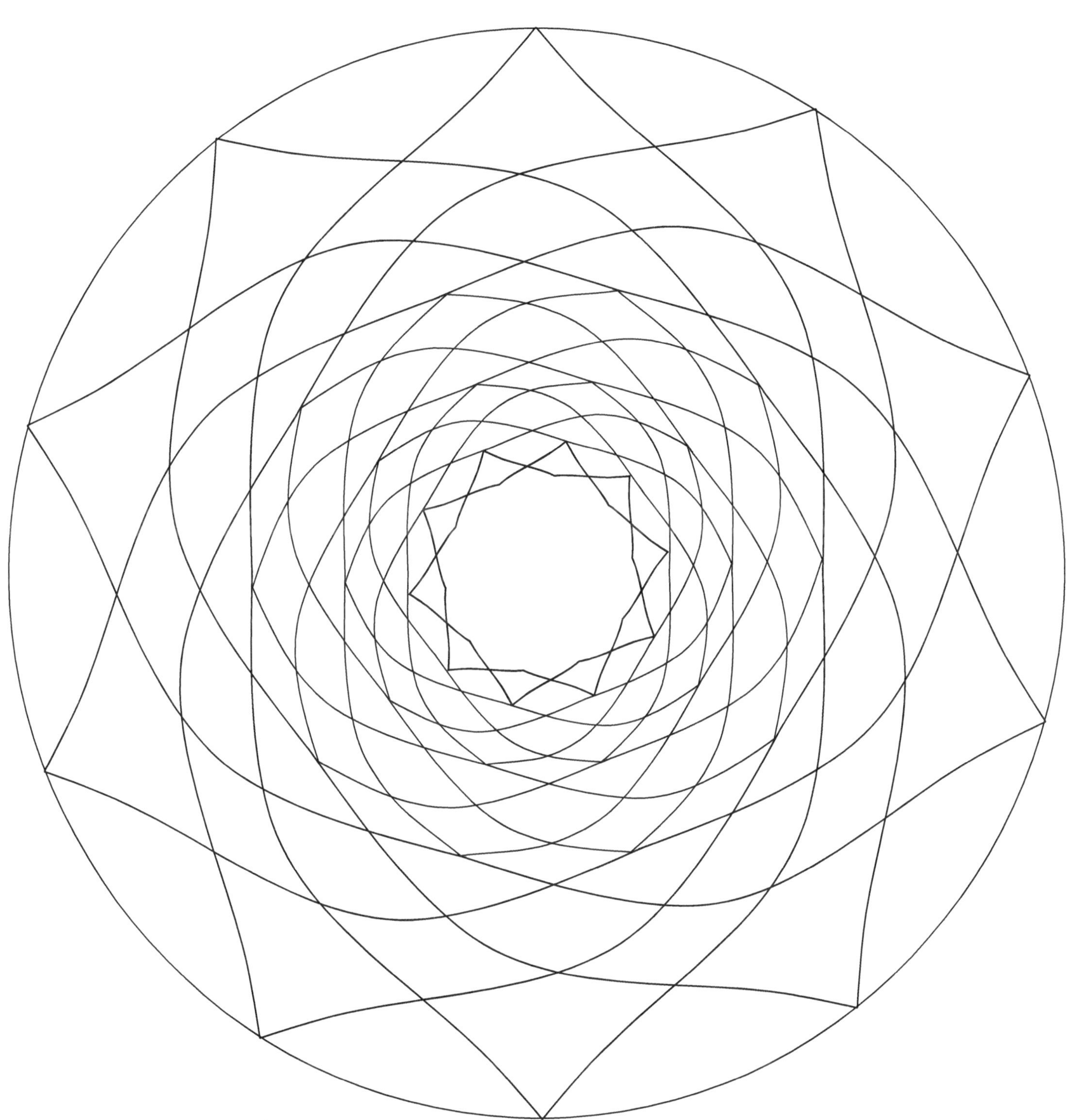

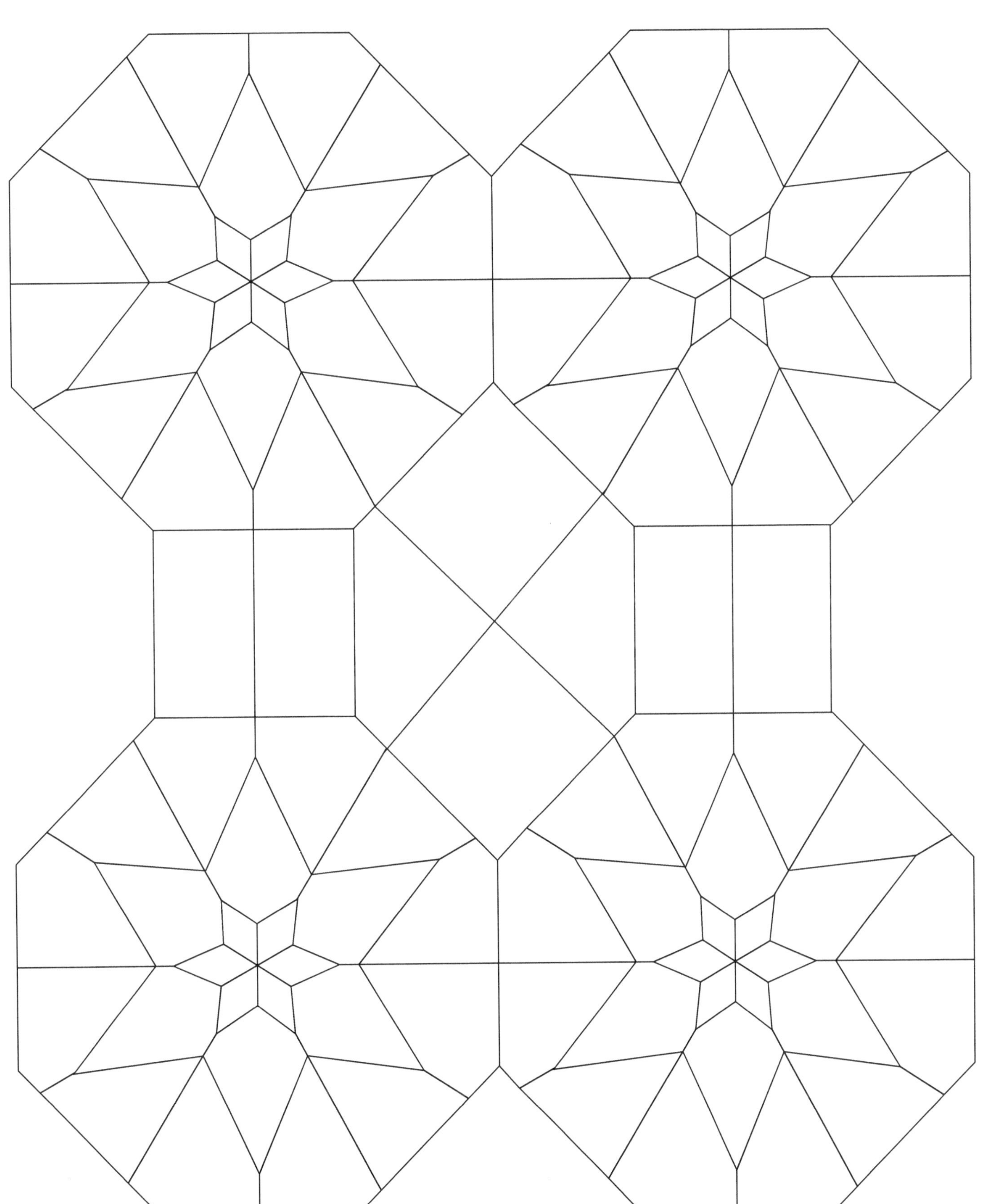

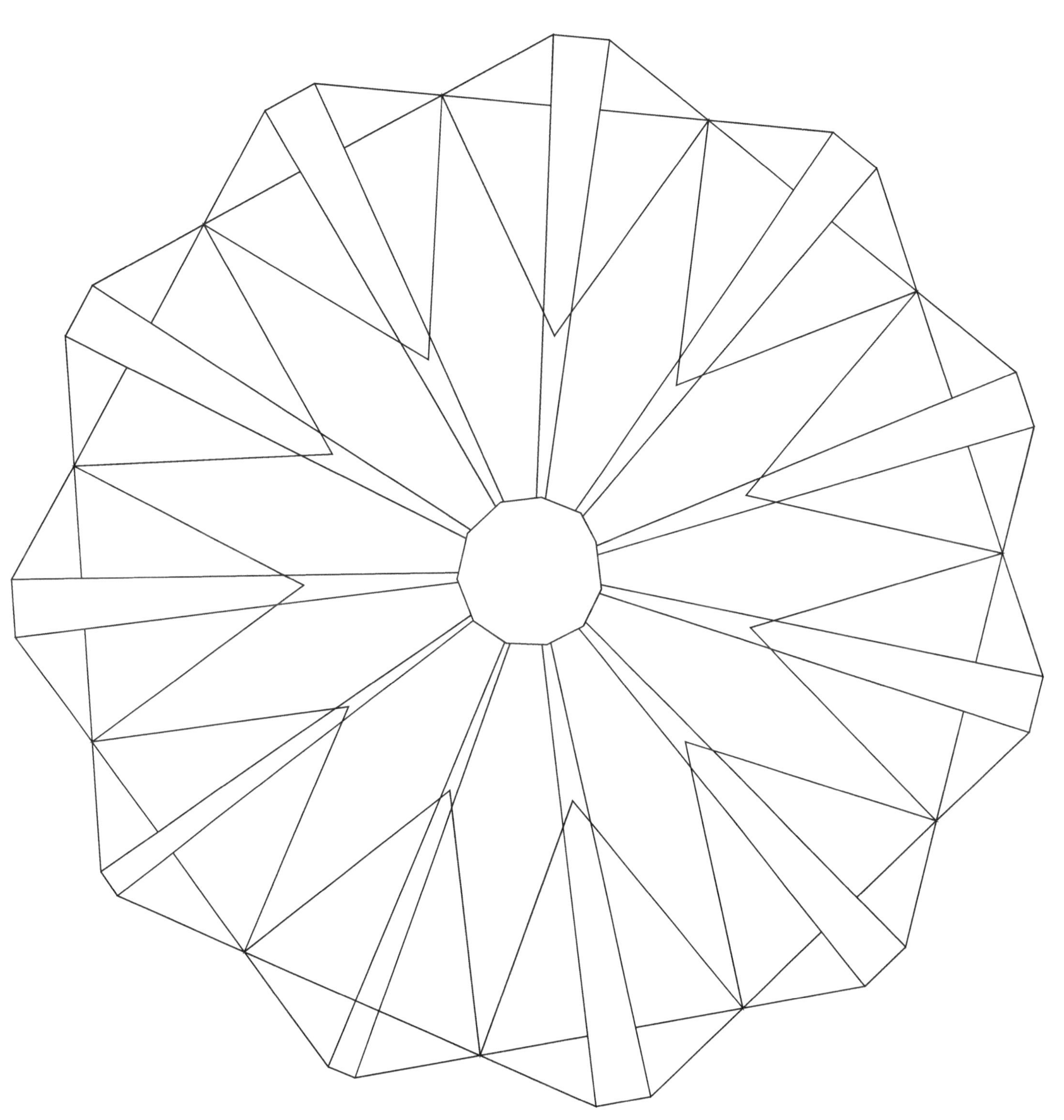

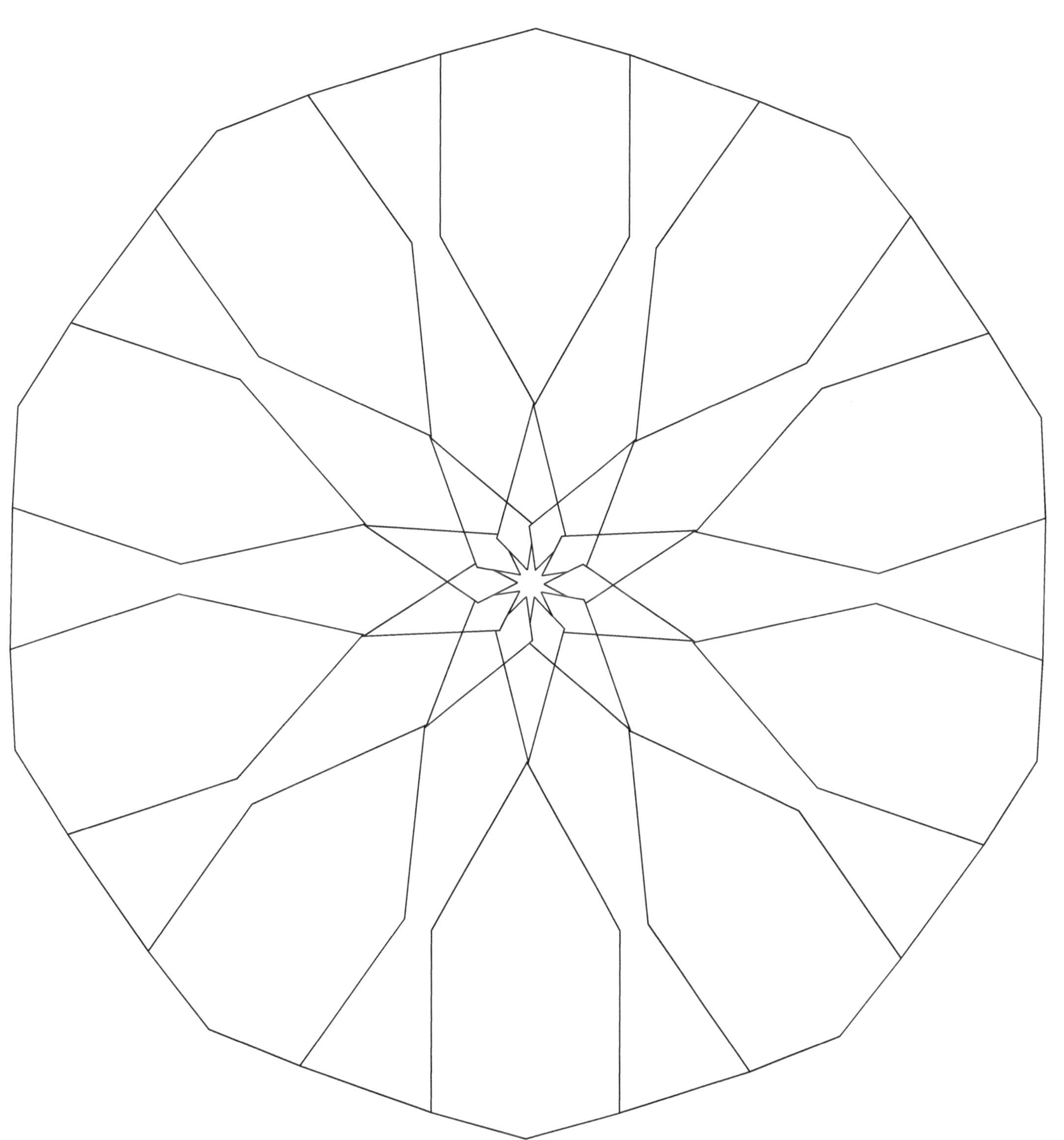

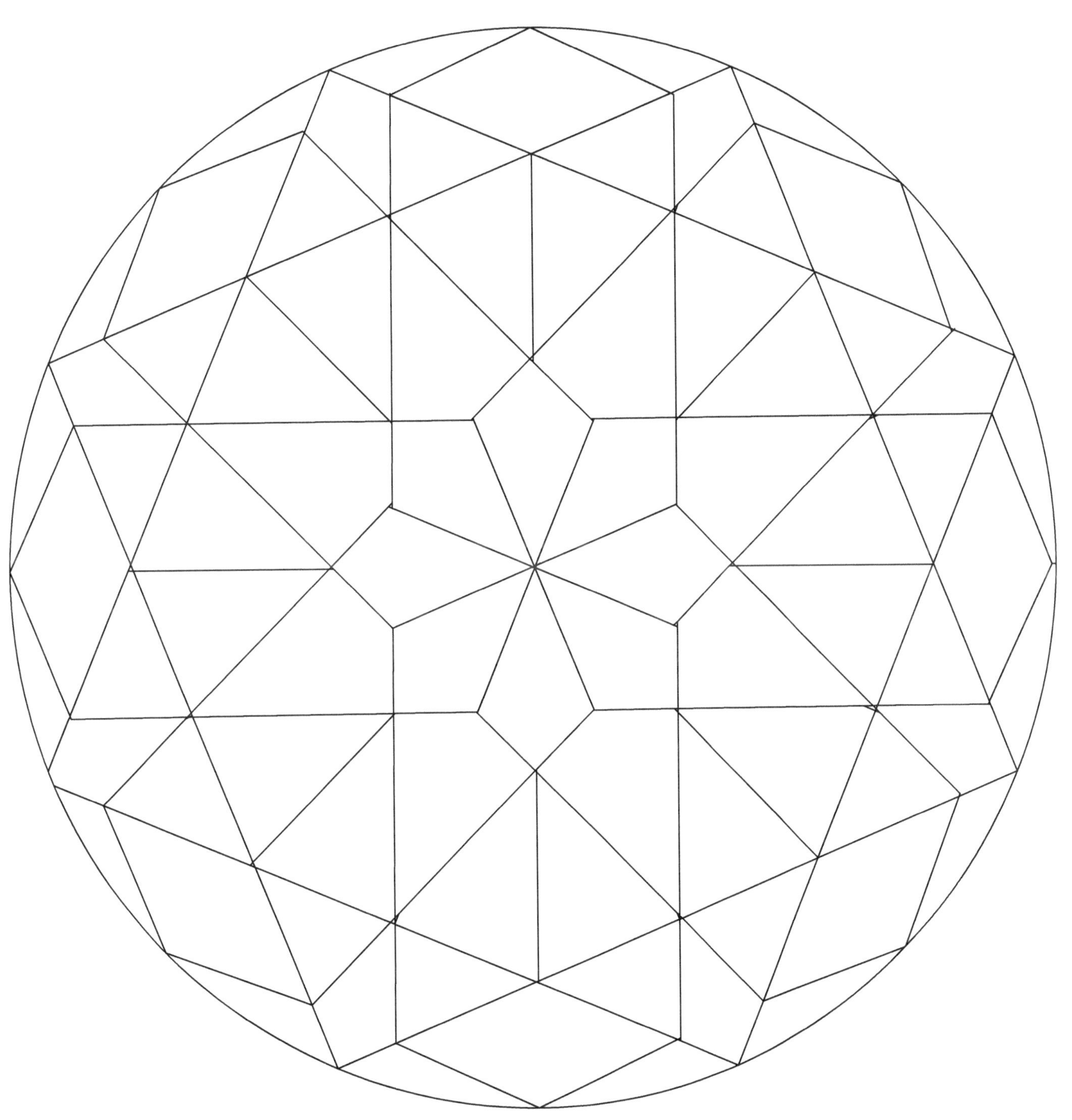